CONTEMPORARY LIVES

JENNIFER LAWRENCE

BREAKOUT ACTRESS

ABDO
Publishing Company

JENNIFER LAWRENCE

BREAKOUT ACTRESS

by Melissa Higgins

CREDITS

Published by ABDO Publishing Company, PO Box 398166, Minneapolis, MN 55439. Copyright © 2013 by Abdo Consulting Group, Inc. International copyrights reserved in all countries. No part of this book may be reproduced in any form without written permission from the publisher. The Essential Library™ is a trademark and logo of ABDO Publishing Company.

Printed in the United States of America,
North Mankato, Minnesota
092012
012013

 THIS BOOK CONTAINS AT LEAST 10% RECYCLED MATERIALS.

Editor: Megan Anderson
Series Designer: Emily Love

Cataloging-in-Publication Data
Higgins, Melissa.
 Jennifer Lawrence: breakout actress / Melissa Higgins.
   p. cm. -- (Contemporary lives)
Includes bibliographical references and index.
ISBN 978-1-61783-620-6
1. Lawrence, Jennifer, 1990- --Juvenile literature. 2. Actors--United States--Biography--Juvenile literature. 1. Title.
791.4302/8092--dc15
[B]

2012945974

TABLE OF CONTENTS

Fans eagerly anticipated Lawrence's debut as Katniss in *The Hunger Games* in March 2012.

CHAPTER 1

Ready for Fame?

||||||||||||||||||||||||||||||||||||

As 21-year-old Jennifer Lawrence sat at a red light near her Santa Monica, California, home, she noticed a billboard she'd seen many times before—but never with a giant picture of her face on it. The black-, red-, and gold-hued advertisement featured her larger-than-life image sighting down an arrow held in a tautly drawn bow. As Lawrence gawked at the billboard, she told herself, "That's

THE HUNGER GAMES NOVELS

The Hunger Games is a trilogy of science fiction adventure novels that begins with narrator Katniss Everdeen's fight for survival after her oppressive government forces her into a game of life or death. The *New York Times* describes Katniss Everdeen as a "memorably complex and fascinating heroine."[2]

Author Suzanne Collins wrote the trilogy, which includes themes such as the effects of war, sacrifice, power, and class struggle. Collins, who began her career as a children's television writer, came up with the idea for the dystopian Hunger Games series while flipping between televised news coverage of the Iraq war and a reality-show talent competition. Collins also drew inspiration from her interest in Greek mythology and the gladiator games of ancient Rome. The three novels in The Hunger Games trilogy include *The Hunger Games* (2008), *Catching Fire* (2009), and *Mockingjay* (2010).

you. Feel it. Feel it."[1] But try as she might, it just wouldn't sink in.

In a few short weeks, the actress would be appearing as Katniss Everdeen in the hotly anticipated film adaptation of Suzanne Collins' best-selling novel *The Hunger Games*. While Lawrence felt unsure about the coming firestorm of publicity, her nervousness wasn't due to a lack of Hollywood experience. Her film-acting résumé included parts in more than ten movies, with a role in the independent film *Winter's Bone* earning her heaps of critical acclaim and a 2011 Academy Award nomination. In the summer of 2011, Lawrence had even appeared in her first major studio release, as Raven/Mystique in the blockbuster superhero-adventure *X-Men: First Class*.

PLAYING A PHENOMENON

Some of Lawrence's unease over her latest role came from her fear of disappointing Hunger Games fans. Lawrence did not hesitate to take the role because of the daunting physical demands of racing through a fiery forest of exploding trees and weeks of archery training. The expectations of fans were the hardest factor for Lawrence as she considered the proposition of playing Katniss. As she explained to one interviewer, "It's not very often you play a role that's famous before you even get there."[3]

And a role couldn't be much more famous than that of Katniss Everdeen. As of March 2012, Scholastic, the publisher of the Hunger Games

> "Listen, I know from the bottom of my heart that I love Katniss. I love her. It's kind of like when you have a huge crush on somebody, and it's almost scary because you don't want to mess it up and have it not be everything you hope it will be. That's exactly what I feel about this. I'm terrified. Is it going to be good enough? Am I going to be good enough?"[4]
>
> —JENNIFER LAWRENCE ON KATNISS EVERDEEN

trilogy, announced that more than 36.5 million copies of the books were in print. By the time the movie premiered in March 2012, the first book (*The Hunger Games*, published in 2008) had been on the *New York Times* bestseller list for three consecutive years. Although written and marketed toward a young adult audience, the novels have appealed to both adults and teens. The combination of ferocious action, a female hero, and an intriguing dystopian universe drew both male and female readers to the books. The Hunger Games trilogy had a large, loyal following.

Lawrence's expectations were even higher because she counted herself among the millions of Hunger Games fans. After her mother recommended them, Lawrence had read and fell in love with all three novels in the series. Lawrence understood the character and knew she was capable of doing her justice.

The filmmakers were glad Lawrence was interested. Director Gary Ross told *Entertainment Weekly* he knew almost instantly that he had found Katniss:

> We had a meeting and I found her to be just a completely compelling, intelligent person. But then she came in and read for me and it just knocked me out. . . . [W]e did a scene from the movie and it was so amazingly powerful that it was sort of stunning. You glimpsed every aspect of the role and the potential of the whole movie.[5]

Lawrence was thrilled when she was offered the role, but she also had reservations. There was a real possibility that if she accepted, she would go from being a respected actor to a cultural phenomenon. Lawrence had tasted media attention after her Academy Award nomination for *Winter's Bone*, but that was a small independent film, not a major studio blockbuster.

"I knew that as soon as I said yes, my life would change," she told *Entertainment Weekly*.[6] She took three days before reaching a decision about the role, thinking over every scenario and listening to advice from family and friends. Ultimately, it came down to her love for the story and the character and knowing she would regret turning down the role.

THE HUNGER GAMES RELEASED

Whether or not Lawrence was ready for the media and fan frenzy, reality began setting in following her encounter with her image on the billboard. The day before *The Hunger Games* premiered on March 12, 2012, at the Nokia Theatre in Los Angeles, California, Lawrence visited fans camped out near the theater. She was blown away as she gazed across the tents, banners, and close to 400 excited fans of the trilogy.

Leading up to the film's release, Lawrence embarked on an eight-city mall tour across the country to promote the movie. Joining her were her *Hunger Games* costars Josh Hutcherson, who

Lawrence traveled across the country with costars Hemsworth, *left*, and Hutcherson, *right*, to promote the film.

plays Peeta Mellark, and Liam Hemsworth, who plays Gale Hawthorne. At every stop, the noise and excitement among fans grew. On March 23, 2012, fans camped out and waited in long lines for the film's midnight opening at more than 4,000 movie screens across the United States.

By now, a very relieved Lawrence had seen the movie and liked it—she knew the film would not let fans down. Moviegoers seemed pleased

On April 2, 2012, 11 days after its March 23 release, *The Hunger Games* reached $253 million in North American ticket sales. Only five other movies had reached the $250-million domestic-ticket-sales milestone within 11 days: *The Dark Knight* (in 8 days), *Harry Potter and the Deathly Hallows: Part 2* (in 9 days), *Transformers: Revenge of the Fallen* (in 9 days), *Pirates of the Caribbean: Dead Man's Chest* (in 10 days), and *Star Wars: Episode III—Revenge of the Sith* (in 11 days).

with the book's film adaptation. The movie spent four consecutive weeks in the number one spot in box-office sales.

Professional reviews of the film were also mostly favorable, especially for Lawrence. Expressing a common sentiment about her performance, Dana Stevens of *Slate* magazine wrote,

> The key to making this adaptation work was the casting of Katniss Everdeen. . . . The film's producers nailed it in picking Jennifer Lawrence . . . who carries the whole film on her sturdy shoulders.[7]

KEEPING IT REAL

Lawrence was accustomed to being in the spotlight for her acting ability even though she had no formal acting training. She had earned awed praise from directors and talent agents since she was discovered at the age of 14 in New York City, New York. But the kind of attention launched by *The Hunger Games* phenomenon was entirely different. Now paparazzi camped out and hid in the bushes near her Santa Monica, California, home. They snapped photos of her shopping at the grocery store and walking down the street with her boyfriend, actor Nicholas Hoult. The explosion of

CRITICAL PRAISE AS KATNISS

Lawrence received critical acclaim for her performance as Katniss in *The Hunger Games*. Peter Travers of *Rolling Stone* wrote, "My advice is to keep your eyes on Lawrence, who turns the movie into a victory by presenting a heroine propelled by principle instead of hooking up with the cutest boy."[8]

Chicago Tribune critic Michael Phillips said, "She doesn't grab the screen like a performer whose mission is to become a movie star. Rather, she acts. Naturally."[9] *New York Magazine*'s David Edelstein wrote: "The actress is not a conventionally chiseled Hollywood ingénue or a trained action star. But there's a steadiness in her [green] eyes that makes her riveting."[10]

gossipy tabloid stories about her in the media tied knots in her stomach.

But the five-foot-nine (1.75 m), green-eyed actress from Louisville, Kentucky, remained determined to stay down-to-earth. With plenty more to explore with Katniss in the three upcoming Hunger Games sequels, Lawrence had also signed on to roles in smaller independent films such as *The Silver Linings Playbook* and *Serena*.

As her star continued rising, plenty of opportunities were opening up for Lawrence to work with directors and actors she greatly admired. Meanwhile, she counted on her friends, and especially her parents and two brothers, to keep her grounded—roles they have played in her life from the very beginning.

||||||||||

Lawrence's *Hunger Games* role brought her international fame.

Jennifer grew up the youngest of three children in Kentucky.

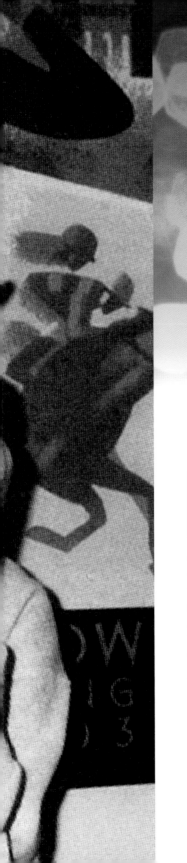

CHAPTER 2

Discovered in the Big Apple

||||||||||||||||||||||||||||||||||||||||||||||||||||||||||||||||||||||||

It seems Jennifer Lawrence has always been a bit of a surprise. Her parents, Karen and Gary, thought they were done having kids after sons Ben and Blaine. They'd even gotten rid of the crib. Then, daughter Jennifer Shrader Lawrence was born on August 15, 1990, the first girl born on her father's side of the family in 50 years.

Growing up on a horse farm, Jennifer did plenty of riding. Her first steed was a cute but mean pony named Muffin. Next came horses Dan and Brumby, who at first hated one another until a big storm scared them into huddling together in the barn. After that, the two horses were inseparable. The horses Jennifer rode weren't always well trained, resulting in her share of riding injuries, including one fall that caused her tailbone to become deformed. She still enjoys riding.

The Lawrences owned a home in Indian Hills, a suburb near Louisville, Kentucky, and a horse farm where Jennifer enjoyed riding. Gary operated a building contracting business and Karen ran Camp Hi-Ho, a summer camp in neighboring Shelby County. Nicknamed "Nitro" by her brothers because she was so hyperactive, Jennifer was raised in the same tough way as her older brothers. In preschool, she got into trouble for playing too roughly with the other girls, so she had to play with the boys instead.

Jennifer vented her rough-and-tumble energy playing field hockey and softball and cheerleading at Kammerer Middle School. She even played on the boys' basketball team her father coached.

At home, her brothers kept their little sister on her toes by including her in their fights and backyard slingshot wars.

When Jennifer wasn't playing, she was often reading or expecting someone to read to her. Jennifer was so obsessed with stories that when she was three years old, she corrected her grandfather after he skipped over details in a story she'd memorized. According to her mom, Jennifer knew she had places to go and had a hard time fitting in with other kids.

||||||||||||||||||||||||||||||||||||||||||||||||||||||||

EARLY LOVE OF ACTING

By the age of five, Jennifer was reciting lines from the Adam Sandler movie *Billy Madison* and acting out the cheerleading skits from *Saturday Night Live*. Her natural acting ability also had its practical side. After getting into trouble for jumping out of a school bus on a dare, she managed to persuade the principal she did it because she was terrified for her life. Her acting was so convincing, not only did she not get suspended, the principal gave her two weeks off from homework due to posttraumatic stress.

Without ever receiving any training, Jennifer discovered her talent for acting at a very young age.

Jennifer's more formal acting roles began at the age of nine, when she played a prostitute from Nineveh at Christ Methodist Church in a play based on the Bible. Jennifer took over the play, swinging her hips and strutting across the stage. She had finally found something that she loved and could connect with—acting.

By age 14, Jennifer had spent a few years on stage, including a semester at the Walden Theatre in Louisville playing Desdemona in Shakespeare's *Othello*. She was in eighth grade and bound for Ballard High School in the fall. But a spring break vacation spent in New York City, New York, changed not only her school plans, but the direction of her life.

"I remember she did a scene from *Othello* and she picked it up very quickly. . . . I knew she was going to go places. I didn't realize it would be so quick but she said, 'I'm going to do this.' . . . I got a sense that she was way more determined than most of the kids her age."[1]

—CHARLIE SEXTON, JENNIFER'S ACTING COACH AT WALDEN THEATRE

THE BIG APPLE

During her school's spring break in 2004, Jennifer and her mom were watching break-dancers perform in New York City's Union Square. A man claiming to be a talent scout for a commercial for clothing retailer H&M approached them, asking if he could take Jennifer's picture. She and her mom agreed, only later considering how bizarre the guy's request was. But the photographer turned out to be legitimate, and soon Jennifer was fielding calls from agents inviting her to interviews. At one agency, she read for a Reese's Peanut Butter Cup commercial, where the agent told her it was the best cold-read they'd ever heard from a 14-year-old.

Karen thought the agent was exaggerating and just being polite. But Jennifer had the overwhelming feeling she was exactly where she needed to be at exactly the right time. She begged her parents—whom she describes as the opposite of stage parents—to let her move to New York City. To bolster her argument, she showed them a local newspaper article about a boy from Kentucky who was starring in a new movie called *Little Manhattan*. The boy, as it turned out, was Josh

> **"I didn't want her to be a diva. I didn't mind if she was girlie, as long as she was tough."[2]**
>
> —*KAREN LAWRENCE*

Hutcherson—who would end up costarring with Jennifer as Peeta in *The Hunger Games*.

Even though they were skeptical their daughter would succeed, her parents finally agreed. They allowed Jennifer to stay in New York for two months over the summer of 2004. Because her mom was busy running the summer camp, Jennifer's brother Blaine, who was 19 years old, moved into an apartment with her.

REAL TALENT?

Jennifer was positive she had found her calling, and she never wanted to look back. Her parents were still unsure. "In our family, everything was about sports," Karen told *Louisville Magazine*. "If she could've thrown a baseball, we would have been able to tell that she could pitch. We just didn't recognize her talent."[3]

Looking for a professional opinion about their daughter's acting ability, the Lawrences arranged for Jennifer to meet with respected acting coach Flo Greenberg. Greenberg was so impressed with Jennifer's talent that she recommended the young actress move forward with pursuing her acting career immediately. Greenberg's advice to Jennifer to move forward without further training was not something she said about many actresses.

Jennifer's two-month New York adventure extended into the fall. Her mom moved in with her, and the offers rolled in. Jennifer landed her very first acting job when she was still only 14, appearing in a promo for the Music Television (MTV) show *My Super Sweet 16*.

|||||||||||||||||||||||||||||||||||||||||||||||||||||||||||||||||||||||||||||

MOVE TO LOS ANGELES

Jennifer flew out to Los Angeles, California, for screen tests and auditions. She would go on to land assignments with clothing brand Abercrombie & Fitch, a commercial for Burger King, and small parts on television series such as *Cold Case*, *Monk*, and *Medium*.

After living in New York City for about a year, Jennifer's gigs in Los Angeles required a cross-country move. As a young teen making her way in acting, a field typically filled with more

A visit to New York City became life changing for Jennifer.

disappointment than success, for Jennifer it was an amazingly easy journey.

Jennifer later joked about the story of how she broke into acting to *Access Hollywood:* "It's one of those stories I don't like telling, because then nobody likes me. It's one of those things that doesn't happen."[4] The acting roles awaiting Jennifer, however, would soon make up for any lack of grittiness in her real life.

||||||||||

The Bill Engvall Show gave Jennifer
her first consistent acting job.

CHAPTER 3
Small and Big Screen Roles

uring 2005 and 2006, Jennifer appeared in photo shoots and accepted small acting jobs, including a small role as Tiff in the movie *Garden Party*. When she wasn't working, Jennifer took online classes to earn her high school diploma. Spending nine hours a day in her room studying was the worst period of her life, but it was the only way her parents would let her continue acting. Attending high school wouldn't have made her any happier, anyway. She'd always felt anxious sitting behind a desk and didn't like comparing herself to other students. Jennifer's hard work paid off when she received her high school diploma at age 16 with a 3.9 grade-point average.

The transition to the Los Angeles area wasn't an easy adjustment for Jennifer, who at first had a hard time making friends. Jennifer missed New York and eventually rented an apartment there for her frequent visits. But the condominium Jennifer shared with her mom in Santa Monica was close to the beach, something she enjoyed. Jennifer eventually found a new group of friends and worked as a nanny for a nine-year-old girl to fill out her time and earn a little money.

"When I started, I had no idea what I was doing, I didn't know what else to do, I didn't know how to act, I just knew how to talk. And I think once I started understanding, I was like, 'Well, I don't really want to learn how to act. I want to just keep learning how to talk.'"[1]

—JENNIFER LAWRENCE ON ACTING

THE BILL ENGVALL SHOW

In 2007, when Jennifer was 15, she landed a job coveted by many actors: a steady role on a television series. The Turner Broadcasting System (TBS) comedy series was called *The Bill Engvall Show*, and Jennifer signed a seven-year contract to play the character Lauren Pearson. Set in a Denver suburb, the half-hour sitcom starred comedian Bill Engvall, who played a family therapist with trouble understanding his own family. Jennifer's character, the oldest of three siblings, was a typical teenage girl dealing with high school and dating.

While Jennifer enjoyed and appreciated her television role and small movie parts, she yearned for a more substantial film role. As long as a movie's filming schedule didn't conflict with her television series, she was allowed to do both. It was an exciting prospect, and Jennifer wanted a part in every script she read. Similar to most young actors, Jennifer auditioned for every part that came her way.

When Jennifer finally landed her first big film role at age 16, the character and material were universes away from *The Bill Engvall Show* and anything she'd ever imagined. "The comedies and the lovey-dovey movies didn't pick me," she told one interviewer. "The dark, dark dramas, the dirty indies picked me."[2]

THE POKER HOUSE

The first dark drama that picked Jennifer was *The Poker House*. In the movie, Jennifer plays Agnes, a 14-year-old tomboy and bookworm who takes care of her two younger sisters while coping with a drug-addicted mom. The film takes place during the course of one day in 1976 in a small Iowa

INDIES

Independent films, nicknamed *indies*, are movies not produced by major film studios, such as Disney, Time-Warner, Twentieth Century Fox, Paramount, or Universal. Independent films are generally produced with low budgets and tend to feature social issues or subjects typically shunned by studios because they can lack appeal to larger mainstream audiences. Although studio features usually pay higher salaries than independent films, indies can offer actors deep, complex roles that showcase their acting abilities. A movie that is well received at festivals can help an actor translate that recognition into higher-paying, more mainstream roles.

town. Agnes's home is a place of prostitution where local men gamble. One of these men sexually abuses Agnes. The story is based on the real-life childhood of the film's writer and director, Lori Petty, an actor who has appeared in many movies including *Free Willy* and *A League of Their Own*. Actor Selma Blair costarred as her mother in the film, which was shot over a 20-day period outside of Chicago during the spring of 2007.

When Jennifer won the role after the audition, she was excited to finally have a major role in a film. At first, Jennifer thought the experience would be fun, but she found leaving the dark, emotional part behind difficult once filming ended.

Even with her loving and stable childhood, Jennifer developed the distinctive ability to access darker places and emotions through her acting. Playing realistic roles in independent movies would become one of her early trademarks—one that she enjoyed.

THE BURNING PLAIN

After filming *The Poker House* in 2007, Jennifer, now 17, went on location to New Mexico for her next movie and her biggest film up to that point, *The Burning Plain*. The film, starring well-known actresses Charlize Theron and Kim Basinger, follows a mix of characters whose lives are seemingly unconnected but are actually joined through time. Jennifer plays Mariana, a troubled teen who catches her mother cheating on her husband, which causes Mariana to fall into a dark romance. As with her role in *The Poker House*,

THE STRESS OF PLAYING A DARK CHARACTER

Jennifer was only 16 years old when she starred in her first movie, *The Poker House*. As a newcomer, Jennifer had yet to learn how to leave her work behind when filming ended. That meant she was unprepared for the emotional toll the role of Agnes would take. Jennifer saw a therapist recommended by a friend for a short while after filming the project. She later told *FilmMaker* magazine:

"I just felt I had to take all of it on, and it did take a toll on me. It's just hard to come out of because you spend two months being a person and going in these dark places, and when you're young you don't know how to get out of those dark places."[3]

her character has to cope with an irresponsible mom while caring for her younger siblings. This would become a recurring theme in many of Jennifer's roles.

The film was the directorial debut of screenwriter Guillermo Arriaga, and expectations were high. With two big-name actresses and a $20-million budget, *The Burning Plain* was anticipated to be a huge success. The movie would help Jennifer be recognized as an emerging talent.

|||||||||||||||||||||||||||||||||||||||||||||||||||||||

PREMIERES AND AWARDS

Both of Jennifer's film projects premiered about a year after they were filmed. *The Poker House* had its first screening at the Los Angeles Film Festival on June 20, 2008, but the film was not widely reviewed. Jennifer's performance as Agnes was singled out, however, and she won the festival's Outstanding Performance Award.

Three months later, *The Burning Plain* premiered at the Venice International Film Festival, the world's oldest film festival. It was held August 27 through September 6, 2008, in Venice, Italy.

FILM FESTIVALS

Film buffs and filmmakers hold film festivals to screen a selection of movies during a single event over a short period of time. Usually held annually, hundreds of festivals taking place all over the world typically feature a particular type or genre of film, such as international, regional, experimental, independent, or science fiction. There's even a festival for films rejected by other film festivals.

Some of the best-known North American film festivals that feature independent movies include the Sundance Film Festival in Park City, Utah; the Toronto International Film Festival in Toronto, Canada; and the Telluride Film Festival in Telluride, Colorado. Festivals provide filmmakers with a way to get their movies seen, with the possibility of reaching a wider audience. Independent films that receive positive reviews and earn a festival's top awards have a chance of catching the attention of film-distribution companies. These companies market the films for a percentage of the profits and get them into mainstream theaters.

Once again, Jennifer's performance impressed judges and earned her the festival's Marcello Mastroianni Award for best emerging performer. The film's premiere was Jennifer's first trip down a red carpet. She and her family took advantage of the event by turning it into their first-ever European vacation. Jennifer told *Flare* magazine:

Lawrence and the *Burning Plain* cast premiered the film at the Venice International Film Festival.

Two weeks beforehand we traveled all around. By the time we got to Venice, we had spent so much time in the same clothes, crammed in a car eating Pringles. And then we got to Venice and all of a sudden we were in ball gowns.[4]

The experience and recognition increased Jennifer's confidence as she pursued her next acting challenge. It would help her land her breakout role and solidify her reputation as a very talented actress.

||||||||||

Lawrence, with costar John Hawkes, *right*, fought hard for her *Winter's Bone* role.

CHAPTER 4

A Breakout Performance

||||||||||||||||||||||||||||||||||||||||||||||||||||||||||||||||||||||||||||

When Jennifer's mother read *Winter's Bone: A Novel*, written by Daniel Woodrell, she told her daughter she would be perfect for the lead role if the book were ever turned into a movie. A few years later, Jennifer received a script based on the book from her agent and immediately thought the character of Ree Dolly was the best female role she'd ever

> "I can't even remember a movie I've seen where a woman is the strong one, a woman is at the forefront of the story and she's not a sidekick to another man who is going on an incredibly difficult journey. And not even a grown woman, [but] a young 17-year-old woman."[1]
>
> —*JENNIFER LAWRENCE ON* WINTER'S BONE

read. It was a rare chance to play a character she truly admired.

In *Winter's Bone*, Ree Dolly is struggling to care for her invalid mother and two younger siblings in the Missouri Ozarks. Ree's father, Jessup, is arrested for making methamphetamine, but he disappears after using the family's house as his bond to get out of jail. When Jessup fails to appear in court, Ree faces the looming threat of losing the house, and she embarks on a torturous backwoods quest to find her father. Ree's clannish relatives complicate her search, particularly her Uncle Teardrop, played by actor John Hawkes, who is angry she's unbalancing their secretive lives.

FIGHTING FOR THE ROLE

Jennifer studied the script and was determined to nab the deep and complex role at her Los Angeles audition. Jennifer made an impression at the audition and was quickly called back for a second interview with the film's director, Debra Granik, and producer Anne Rosellini. Granik and Rosellini had cowritten the screenplay.

Granik's goal was to keep the movie as authentic as possible. The character of Ree appears in every scene of the movie. The role required an actor capable of portraying her resiliency and toughness, as well as her caring and protectiveness for her family. But the actor needed to also portray a young woman born and raised in the Ozark Mountain region convincingly. The filmmakers liked Jennifer, who stood out at her reading with her Kentucky accent. "For the first time I felt like

"I love movies with teeth. I love movies that make you think. I love movies that are going to challenge me in all different colors and ways I've never done."[2]

—LAWRENCE ON PICKING ROLES

> "I've just always had this attitude of don't stop until you get it. I did just kind of have . . . that dumb, naive attitude of, 'Well, I want it!' And then when you get told no, just saying, 'Well, no, I'm going to get it, with or without you.'"[4]
>
> —*JENNIFER LAWRENCE*

I was really hearing Ree," Granik told *Louisville Magazine*.[3]

But Granik also had a clear vision of Ree's physical appearance and felt that Jennifer didn't quite match that vision because she was too pretty. Granik and Rosellini flew to New York City to audition more actors for the part.

Jennifer, who had grown obsessed with winning the role, was disappointed yet undeterred upon learning why she was turned down for the part. In a display of Ree-worthy stubbornness, Jennifer took a red-eye flight from Los Angeles to New York to make a last-ditch effort at auditioning for Granik. Jennifer arrived at the audition tired and disheveled. She was not wearing any makeup and had not washed her hair or face. After about 15 minutes of performing improvisation for

Granik, they had a lengthy discussion about the project. To Jennifer's great relief and excitement, she was selected for the role of Ree.

||||||||||||||||||||||||||||||||||||||||||||||||||||||||||

A TOUGH SHOOT

Filming for *Winter's Bone* was scheduled over 25 days during February and March 2009, when Lawrence was 18. It would be shot entirely on location, without the use of sets, throughout Greene, Taney, and Christian Counties in Missouri. Because of Granik's emphasis on realism, she asked Lawrence to spend time on location to develop an

ACTING METHOD ||||||||||||||||||||||||||||||||||||||||||||||||||||||||||||||||||||

When preparing for a movie shoot, Lawrence reads her lines once or twice, memorizes them, and comes to set. Her acting is instinctual. After her difficult *Poker House* role, she learned to separate herself from the characters she plays by making sure the emotions belong to her character and not to her. She uses her imagination to reach feelings she's never personally experienced.

Winter's Bone costar John Hawkes said of Lawrence's acting method, "She's not a person who lives the character 24 hours a day. She has a different way of working than I do that allows her to access emotions. I don't want to say it's easy for her, but she makes it appear easy."[5]

Lawrence immersed herself in the location and wardrobe to get into her character.

understanding of the people and learn about their daily lives. Lawrence soaked up the surroundings of the region by living in the Ozarks for two weeks before filming began. In particular, she spent time with the family who lived in what would be used as Ree's house in the film. Lawrence's training for the role also included learning how to chop wood, handle a rifle, and skin and cook a squirrel for dinner.

Lawrence also inhabited the role of Ree Dolly physically. She had her teeth painted yellow and wore minimal makeup on her face and lips, which chapped from the cold. A wardrobe that included bulky jackets, a wool cap, and flannel shirts also helped her get into her character. The film included a scene where Lawrence cuts open a squirrel, but the only way she could do it was by immersing herself completely into her character's mindset. Once the director called "Cut!" Lawrence came out of her character, shrieking and jumping around.

It was a tough shoot with long hours, night shoots, and hard work created by the film's dark material and uncompromising realism. During filming, the weather in the Ozarks region fluctuated between too cold and too hot. Having turned 18 before filming began, it was also Lawrence's first movie shoot without either of her parents on set. When she was struck with homesickness, Lawrence asked her parents for company, and both her mom and dad joined her in Missouri.

Even though filming *Winter's Bone* had its difficult moments, the cast and crew had fun and

While preparing for her role as Ree in *Winter's Bone*, Lawrence slipped into her native Kentucky accent every time she tried to sound like a Missourian. Afraid it would sound horrible on film, she was relieved when Granik told her she could keep her Kentucky accent. Lawrence called her mom every day, spoke with her for five minutes, and the accent stuck for the entire day.

grew close. "This is the only movie I've ever done where I literally know every single person in the credits," Lawrence told *FilmIndependent*. "I know them personally. We really became a family."[6] In fact, costar Lauren Sweetser, who portrays Ree's best friend, Gail, became Lawrence's real-life best friend.

THE BEAVER

When she returned to Los Angeles, Lawrence taped her third season of *The Bill Engvall Show*, which aired during the summer of 2009. In September, TBS announced the series would not be renewed for a fourth season. Lawrence had mixed feelings about the cancellation. She learned a lot while acting on the series. But the early ending of her seven-year contract meant she was able to take on more film projects without worrying if they conflicted with the show's taping schedule. And since she was becoming an even more sought-after actress, the timing couldn't have been better.

After *Winter's Bone*, Lawrence was ready for a normal role that didn't require skinning squirrels. She wanted something that was a little funnier. *The Beaver* fit that bill perfectly.

The Beaver is a comedy-drama starring Mel Gibson and Jodie Foster, who also directed the film. Gibson plays Walter Black, a depressed man who finds a beaver hand puppet, which he uses as his sole form of communication while he tries to get his life back on track. Lawrence plays Norah, who is a classmate of Walter's son, Porter, played by Anton Yelchin. Norah and Porter develop a relationship and fall in love.

Foster had seen Lawrence in *Winter's Bone* and had typecast her in darker roles. But in a follow-up interview, Lawrence demonstrated her comedic chops by telling Foster a few jokes.

Filmed at the end of 2009, the filming experience was a blast for Lawrence.

Lawrence's performance in *Winter's Bone* would soon put her in the spotlight.

Lawrence has noted that her roles tend to coincide with her life. When filming *The Burning Plain*, much like her character Mariana, she was transitioning from a teenager into a woman. In *Winter's Bone*, similar to Ree Dolly's willingness to sacrifice anything for her family, Lawrence was willing to do anything to win the role. Lawrence has faced overwhelming publicity and a media frenzy surrounding *The Hunger Games*, similar to the way her character, Katniss Everdeen, is unwillingly thrust into the spotlight.

The 19-year-old especially enjoyed working with Foster, considering her to be one of the most real, down-to-earth people she'd ever met, even with her status in the film industry. They both shared the philosophy that acting is a job, and it is important to remain grounded. It was a belief Lawrence would put into practice as her star continued rising.

|||||||||||

Winter's Bone received praise at the 2010 Sundance Film Festival.

CHAPTER 5

From Gritty to Glam

||||||||||||||||||||||||||||||||||||||||||||||

When *Winter's Bone* was accepted into the 2010 Sundance Film Festival, the honor was so unexpected Lawrence cried when she found out. Competition for the prestigious festival is intense. During the 2012 festival, for example, Sundance selected only 117 feature-length films out of 4,042 entries.

Winter's Bone premiered January 21, 2010, and quickly became a Sundance favorite. Even without the attachment of big-name stars, word-of-mouth from festivalgoers made it a must-see entry. The film also dazzled the judges, who awarded *Winter's Bone* the Grand Jury Prize for Drama.

The film and Lawrence, its little-known star, won over critics. The *New York Times* raved, "It is straightforward and suspenseful, but also surprising and subtle . . . [with] as memorable and vivid a heroine as you are likely to see on screen this season."[1]

"In Lawrence, Granik has found just the right young actress to inhabit Ree," extolled *Rolling Stone*. "Her performance is more than acting, it's a gathering storm. . . . *Winter's Bone* is unforgettable. It means to shake you, and does."[2]

TOUGH GIRL OR GIRLY GIRL?

When asked by an interviewer if she felt more comfortable playing a tough girl or a feminine girl, Lawrence's answer displays her resistance against being pigeonholed as an actress:

"I don't know. My voice is deeper, so I'm probably more believable as a tough girl. I don't really think I'm one or the other. I mean, I'm a good driver but I still scream at spiders."[3]

Lawrence was proud of the attention the film was receiving, particularly since she didn't have very high expectations of it reaching a large audience. Lawrence was being called a breakout star and the "next big thing" in the media.[4] While her name began circulating as an Academy Award nominee, the possibility left Lawrence aghast.

"I have no idea how to talk about an Oscar at 20 years old. I can, like, make a dentist appointment, barely."[5]

—JENNIFER LAWRENCE

The same day *Winter's Bone* won at Sundance, Roadside Attractions picked up the film for distribution. The company released it into theaters in June 2010. Buzz about the breakout star increased over the rest of the year as the film found a larger and larger audience. Luckily for Lawrence, she had some new projects to keep her mind off the uncomfortable attention—including a dramatic alteration of her mountain-girl image.

> "The funny thing about Jennifer is that she is nothing like the persona she projects on-screen at all. There's not much serious there. She is as normal as they come and she never stops being funny. She was just born with that deep stare."[7]
>
> —JODIE FOSTER

MIXING THINGS UP

Winter's Bone was the Lawrence film on everyone's minds. Lawrence feared she might be typecast in gritty, independent movie roles, so she decided to make a bold move to counteract the flannel-shirted, woolen-capped image of Ree Dolly. When she was 19, she posed in a bathing suit for a sexy shoot in the June 2010 issue of *Esquire* magazine. As she explained to one interviewer,

> *"I would like to move on to do something different. Have a bigger trailer. Maybe wear makeup in a movie. I mean, that'd just be crazy, right? Me wearing makeup in a movie? Imagine the possibilities!"[6]*

In early summer 2010, Lawrence filmed a supporting role in the film *Like Crazy*, starring

Felicity Jones and Yelchin, Lawrence's *The Beaver* costar. In *Like Crazy*, Lawrence plays Sam, a love interest of Yelchin's character Jacob, who is struggling with a different cross-continent relationship. About a month later, Lawrence shot a horror-thriller, *House at the End of the Street*. The film is about a mother, played by Elisabeth Shue, and her teenage daughter, Lawrence, who move into a house across the street from where a double murder took place.

> "They're really proud of me, and they know I'm doing what I was made to do. . . . So they're very supportive of me. And they're actually very supportive of the *Esquire* shoot, too, because they knew why I was doing it—to avoid being typecast as the girl from *Winter's Bone*."[8]
>
> —JENNIFER LAWRENCE ON HER PARENTS

It was Lawrence's next film that would be her first blockbuster role. She'd finally get that big trailer—and a lot more makeup.

X-MEN: FIRST CLASS

Lawrence partially credits her *Esquire* photo shoot with helping her land a role in her first major studio feature, *X-Men: First Class*. In the movie, she plays young Raven Darkholme, a mutant who becomes the shape-shifter Mystique. It is a role actor Rebecca Romijn originated in three previous X-Men movies: *X-Men* (2000), *X2* (2003), and *X-Men: The Last Stand* (2006).

In *X-Men: First Class*, a prequel to the X-Men movies, the mutants are recruited by the US government in 1962 to foil a fiendish plot threatening to start World War III. The film also explores how the mutants found their powers. Raven/Mystique struggles with blending in with society or embracing her mutantness.

FIRST BIG-BUDGET MOVIE

In most respects, the *X-Men* filming experience couldn't have been more different from *Winter's Bone*. Backed by a major film studio, Twentieth Century Fox, the blockbuster's estimated

$160-million budget eclipsed the estimated $2-million *Winter's Bone* budget.

But in other ways, shooting *X-Men* was the same as every other movie she'd made. "It's still showing up to work on time with your lines memorized, being prepared, and between 'action' and 'cut' listening to the director," she told an interviewer. "My job, the work part of it, is all the same."[9]

BLLIMM BLOCKBUSTER

Today, *blockbuster* refers to a type, or genre, of movie—mainly action-adventure and/or science fiction—released during the summer months to attract large, and mostly young, audiences. The word has a rather fearsome background. First coined in the 1940s during World War II, it described large aerial bombs that could destroy an entire block of buildings. Blockbuster first referred to any film that had "block-busting" success, such as the classic *Gone With the Wind* (1939). With the gargantuan success of the action movie *Jaws* in June 1975, the word took on its more modern connotation. *X-Men: First Class* can be classified as a blockbuster, as can *The Hunger Games*, even though it goes against the blockbuster norm because of its release in the spring rather than the summer. It is also not uncommon for movies that are dubbed blockbusters to fail at the box office.

And, like her role as Ree in *Winter's Bone*, some preparation was required. Lawrence worked out two hours a day, bulking up her muscles with weight training, kicking, and fighting. She also stuck to a high-protein diet. Although she didn't have to perform many of the stunts in the movie, Lawrence still needed to look the part of a well-muscled superhero—especially because she spent half of her screen time with no clothes on, wearing full-body paint as the mutant Mystique.

During the fall 2010 shoot, Lawrence fell in love with London and the English countryside. She had an apartment located in London's funky

MUTANT TRANSFORMATION

Combining five layers of airbrushed paint, five layers of splatter paint, and hand-glued scales, it took a seven-member makeup team six to eight hours to transform Lawrence into Mystique. During some parts of the full-body transformation and while waiting for the makeup to dry, Lawrence could only sit on a bicycle seat or stand. "It was like a really bizarre sleepover where I was just standing up naked being painted and scaled and glued," Lawrence told *Entertainment Weekly*. "There were so many points where I'd think, 'There is nobody else in the whole world who is doing this right now.'"[10] She bonded with her crew, and they would watch movies and television shows to help pass the time.

Lawrence spent eight hours in makeup to transform into shape-shifter Mystique.

Notting Hill neighborhood, and enjoyed shopping and sightseeing with costar and new best friend Zoe Kravitz. Lawrence's experience in England would turn out to be rather relaxed compared to the flurry of excitement that awaited her back in the United States.

||||||||||

In 2011, Lawrence became the second-youngest actress to receive an Oscar nomination for Best Actress.

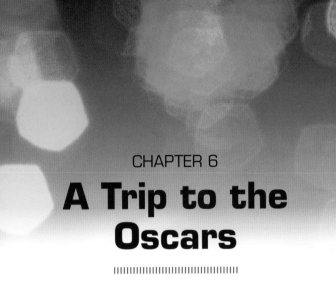

CHAPTER 6

A Trip to the Oscars

||||||||||||||||||||||||||||||||||||||||||||||

By the end of 2010, Jennifer Lawrence was receiving more and more notice for her performance in *Winter's Bone*. In October 2010, *Variety* named her one of 2010's Top Ten Actors to Watch. She was being profiled in magazines and interviewed in newspapers. Summarizing Lawrence's journey into celebrity was the title of the January 19, 2011, cover story of the *Hollywood Reporter*: "Jennifer Lawrence: The Making of an 'It' Actress."

Lawrence returned from filming *X-Men* in England just as movie awards season started heating up in the United States. She would not be missed by two of the biggest award honors. On December 14, 2010, Lawrence received a Golden Globe nomination for Best Performance by an Actress in a Motion Picture–Drama. Two days later, on December 16, the Screen Actors Guild (SAG) nominated Lawrence for Outstanding Performance by a Female Actor in a Leading Role.

The recognition was amazing for a young actress who'd pursued a gritty role in a low-budget film because she'd fallen in love with the character. And the accolades for Lawrence's performance weren't over yet. Many industry insiders were

"To be honest, it's not that I'm not enjoying all of this, I am, I'm having fun. It's just that this weird thing is happening, this shift where people start talking differently, treating me differently or something."[1]

—*JENNIFER LAWRENCE*

Lawrence was recognized with nominations from several major award ceremonies, including the Golden Globes.

certain Lawrence would be nominated for the biggest acting award of them all—an Oscar.

||||||||||||||||||||||||||||||||||||||||||||||||||||

OSCAR NOMINATION

A newcomer to all of the often-uncomfortable media attention, Lawrence tried to remain

ACADEMY AWARDS ||||||||||||||||||||||||||||||||||||||||||||||||||||||||||

The Academy of Motion Picture Arts and Sciences, located in Beverly Hills, California, presents the Academy Awards annually. Founded in 1927, membership to the Academy is by invitation only. Academy members with expertise in a particular area of filmmaking select the nominees in each of the 24 award categories. That means, for example, only directors can nominate directors and actors can nominate actors. The entire Academy membership votes for Best Picture nominees and the final winners.

To be eligible for an Academy Award, a film must be shown for paid admission in a Los Angeles area theater for a minimum of one week between January 1 and December 31 of the year prior to the Awards ceremony. The requirements can differ for some types of films. The award ceremony is held in February or early March. No one is completely sure how the iconic gold-plated award statuette, "Oscar," got its nickname. Oscar weighs 8.5 pounds (3.8 kg) and stands 13.5 inches (34.3 cm) tall.

grounded and take all of the buzz surrounding her in stride. She told one interviewer,

> *Mostly, I'm just really happy that I've been able to do what I love. I know that sounds kind of simple, but I've found something I really love doing and I can do it every day of my life.*[2]

Lawrence slept soundly the night before the 83rd Academy Award nominations announcement on January 25, 2011. The way she saw it, there really wasn't anything to be nervous about. It would be a thrill and an honor if it happened. But she was only 20, and with all of the veteran actresses in her category, she doubted she'd receive a Best Actress Oscar nomination.

Despite her skepticism, Lawrence invited her family and some of her friends over to her Santa Monica condominium at 8:30 a.m. to watch the televised announcement. Wearing her pajamas and bathrobe, Lawrence and her guests gathered around the television.

Before the nominations in Lawrence's category came the nominations for Best Actor in a Supporting Role. Lawrence's cool facade vanished when the presenter read the nomination for John Hawkes, her *Winter's Bone* costar. Lawrence screamed with excitement, but then a hush fell over the living room as the nominees for Best Actress in a Leading Role were about to be announced. When the announcer read her name, "I kind of freaked out a little bit," Lawrence told one interviewer.[3]

"It's embarrassing. I fully went for it. I was jumping up and down, squealing, smiling, hugging my mom. I did the whole thing. I was just a cliché. I thought maybe I would act cool and be like, all right, good cool. . . . Yeah, no, I went full female."[4]

—*JENNIFER LAWRENCE ON REACTING TO HER OSCAR NOMINATION*

The excitement in the room continued as *Winter's Bone* received two additional nominations, for Best Picture and Adapted Screenplay. Lawrence became the second-youngest actress to receive a lead-actress Oscar nomination, next to Keisha Castle-Hughes, who was nominated for *Whale Rider* in 2004 when she was only 13.

OSCAR NIGHT

Actress Natalie Portman was considered a sure thing to win the Oscar that year, for *Black Swan*. Portman had already won both the Golden Globe and Screen Actors Guild awards for her performance. But a few industry insiders were predicting an upset win for Lawrence. "Lawrence is the kind of actress people want to like," said Melena Ryzik of the *New York Times*. "Her performance is so unvarnished. It's against type for a pretty young actress, which is what the industry likes."[5]

Leading up to Oscar night, Lawrence joked with interviewers that instead of an acceptance speech, she was practicing her losing face. More often than not when asked about the Oscars, she would uncomfortably smile and change the subject.

THE COMPETITION

Lawrence's Academy Awards competition for Best Actress in a Leading Role included Annette Bening (*The Kids Are All Right*), Nicole Kidman (*Rabbit Hole*), Michelle Williams (*Blue Valentine*), and Natalie Portman (*Black Swan*). *Winter's Bone* lost to *The King's Speech* for Best Picture, and Hawkes lost to Christian Bale (*The Fighter*) for Best Actor in a Supporting Role.

When asked by *Access Hollywood* if she'd thought about the dress she'd wear to the Academy Awards, Lawrence joked, "I want to wear the Golden Globes dress. What if I cut the straps off or something, just to make it different?"[6] Instead, she wore a sleek and simple red Calvin Klein Collection dress designed by Francisco Costa. The *Los Angeles Times* applauded Lawrence's stroll down the red carpet, "looking stunning and totally understated. Not only is the dress simple, her hair is long, loose and casual and she isn't sporting any major bling at all, just a thin gold bangle on one arm."[7]

On Sunday, February 27, 2011, Lawrence was the first nominated actor to stride down the red carpet at the Kodak Theatre in Los Angeles for the 83rd Academy Awards. One on-air commentator said she looked so gorgeous and flawless that she set the bar high for the celebrities who followed her down the red carpet. Lawrence answered interviewers' questions with her usual joking and self-deprecating charm. She said she was more worried about how to get her friends and family to the same party than what she might say if she won the award.

Lawrence strolled the Oscars red carpet in a stunning red Calvin Klein dress.

Even though Lawrence was herself becoming a celebrity, she was still starstruck. She met actor Josh Brolin at the American Film Institute luncheon in January 2011 and said she couldn't help flirting because he was so cute. She also said she couldn't have a conversation with veteran actor Jeff Bridges because she was such a huge fan. And after talking to Steven Spielberg for ten minutes, she said she got into her car and sobbed, "Because what else do you do when you have a conversation with Steven Spielberg?"[8]

As most people predicted, Portman ended up winning the Oscar. But Lawrence said she enjoyed the experience, particularly watching the musical performance by Florence and the Machine and exchanging disbelieving glances with her dad, who was sitting next to her. After the ceremony, Lawrence attended the *Vanity Fair* after-party but stayed for only 15 minutes.

Lawrence did receive acting honors from at least ten organizations and festivals for her *Winter's Bone* performance. Those honors included the Hollywood Awards, where she accepted the New Hollywood Award from Foster, the Gotham Awards, Young Artist Awards, National Board of Review USA, Palm Springs International Film Festival, and Chicago Film Critics Association.

A few days after walking down the Oscars red carpet, Lawrence took a much-needed weeklong vacation in London. While there, Lawrence would receive the phone call of a lifetime.

ⅠⅠⅠⅠⅠⅠⅠⅠⅠⅠ

Lawrence headed into the woods to film *The Hunger Games*.

CHAPTER 7

Taking on *The Hunger Games*

||||||||||||||||||||||||||||||||||||||||||||||||||||||||||||||||||||||||||||||||||||||||||

Within the span of one month, 21-year-old Lawrence not only attended the Oscars but also landed one of the most coveted roles among Hollywood actresses in her age group. The role was headstrong, bow-and-arrow-wielding heroine Katniss Everdeen in *The Hunger Games*.

Lawrence fell in love with the Hunger Games trilogy after reading the books. She raced through the series in less than four days. She particularly admired Katniss's mental toughness and her focus on surviving rather than choosing a boyfriend. After meeting with the director, Gary Ross, she liked his plans and vision for the movie. And

THE HUNGER GAMES SYNOPSIS

In *The Hunger Games*, Lawrence plays the lead character Katniss Everdeen, a headstrong 16-year-old girl who takes care of her younger sister, Prim, and her widowed mother. Set in the future, the family lives in the impoverished District 12 of Panem, a nation built on the postapocalyptic remains of North America. It is controlled by a totalitarian government called The Capitol. As punishment for a previous rebellion and to discourage further unrest, The Capitol holds an annual competition called the Hunger Games. One boy and one girl from each district are selected as tributes at a Reaping, where names are drawn via a lottery. Prim is selected, and Katniss volunteers to take her place. The 24 tributes travel to the Capitol, where they are interviewed on live television and trained to fight in the competition. The tributes are placed in a high-tech arena and forced to fight one another to the death on live television broadcast throughout Panem. Only one of the tributes can make it out alive and be crowned victor. Katniss and Peeta, the District 12 male tribute, face long odds inside the arena, where they form a tentative alliance and struggle to win against better-trained opponents.

when she learned the trilogy's author, Collins, was working on the screenplay, Lawrence felt even more confident that the movie would do the book justice.

From the director's perspective, Ross believed the right actor for the role of Katniss Everdeen needed to convey a combination of vulnerability and strength, yet be young enough to play a teenager. A number of actresses were in the running for the role, including Abigail Breslin (*Little Miss Sunshine*), Shailene Woodley (*The Descendants*), and Hailee Steinfeld (*True Grit*). But when he met Lawrence, fresh off her Oscar nomination, Ross knew he'd found Katniss. "There was such a power and an intensity and a command [about her]," he told *The Hollywood Reporter*. "I was floored."[1]

LANDING THE ROLE OF KATNISS

Lawrence was vacationing in England after the Oscars when she got a phone call in the middle of the night that the role of Katniss was hers—if she wanted it. As she told one interviewer, she found

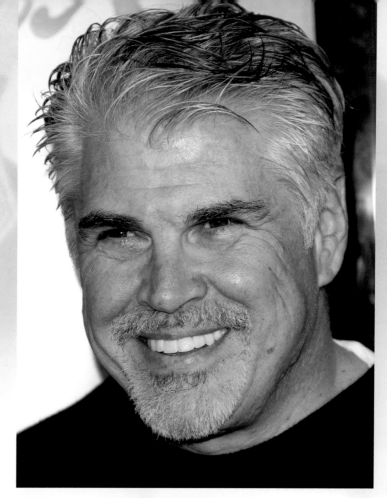

In Lawrence, *Hunger Games* director Ross was confident he had found the right person to play Katniss.

it strange to be considering such a coveted role. It was a part that within just a year could make her arguably the most famous actress her age. She was just getting a taste of fame from *Winter's Bone*. Lawrence decided to take three days to think over her decision about the part. At one point, she found herself sitting in a quiet London coffee shop, unrecognized by other patrons. Lawrence realized the part would make her so instantly recognizable that people would be taking her picture with their phones wherever she went.

But Lawrence didn't want to look back and realize she turned the role down out of fear. Lawrence loved the script. She had so much respect for the character that she knew she was capable of playing the part right. Finally, she accepted. In March 2011, Lionsgate, the studio making and distributing *The Hunger Games*, officially announced who would play Katniss Everdeen: Jennifer Lawrence.

||||||||||||||||||||||||||||||||||||||||||||||||||||||||

VOTE OF CONFIDENCE

Fans had been debating who should be cast as Katniss ever since 2009, when they learned the books would be made into movies. They flooded the Internet with reactions to the news of Lawrence's casting, and not all of the opinions were positive. One common complaint was that 20-year-old Lawrence was too old to play 16-year-old Katniss. Fans also took issue with the

Collins created a worldwide phenomenon with her Hunger Games trilogy and its strong heroine, Katniss.

fact that Lawrence didn't exactly resemble Katniss's olive-skinned, brown-haired description in the books. The naturally blonde Lawrence was too tall, too pretty, and not thin enough.

Among the people confident with the decision was the woman who created Katniss, Collins. Collins had attended every audition for the role of Katniss. Regarding Lawrence's age, Collins believed the actress who played Katniss needed to have a certain level of maturity and power. The character is forced to grow up fast without a father, fight for her survival, and ends up inciting a revolution. Collins also felt there was some flexibility regarding Katniss' race and physical characteristics.

After the audition process, Collins believed Lawrence was the only actress who truly captured the character of Katniss. Collins was so pleased when Lawrence accepted the role that she gave Lawrence a congratulatory phone call, saying, "I feel like when you said yes, the world got lifted off my shoulders."[2]

With the rest of the cast set, *The Hunger Games* was ready to begin filming on May 23, 2011, in the Blue Ridge Mountains near Asheville, North Carolina. But first came Lawrence's preparations for her role.

TRAINING TO BE KATNISS

Lawrence was still in strong physical condition after shooting *X-Men: First Class*. But now she had to shift her goal from bulking up her muscles to becoming fast and lean. Compared to Raven/Mystique, Katniss was younger, faster, and more athletic. Katniss was also an expert with a bow and arrow, a skill Lawrence did not possess. The actress required training to play a skilled hunter such as Katniss convincingly. Her training program consisted of six weeks of archery practice, running that included speed drills, rock climbing, jumping, combat, stunt training, and yoga. Lawrence's archery coach was a four-time Olympian from Eastern Europe. It took several weeks of consistent practice, but eventually Lawrence was capable of hitting the bull's-eye approximately 50 percent of the time.

Lawrence had her usual first-day jitters before the filming of *The Hunger Games* began. But once the shoot began, Lawrence settled in to

POTENTIAL DISASTER |||||||||||||||||||||||||||||||||||||||||||||||||||||||||||||

A few days before *The Hunger Games* filming began, potential disaster struck. Part of Lawrence's training for the film included wall runs, where she practiced running toward a wall as fast as she could to gain the momentum needed to propel her up. During one run, however, Lawrence's stomach struck the wall before her foot. Her trainer thought she might have ruptured her spleen. Lawrence was rushed to the hospital, where a computerized axial tomography (CAT) scan revealed bad bruising. Luckily, nothing was broken. To everyone's relief, filming went on as scheduled.

the six-day-a-week schedule and would have no problem making friends on set.

LOCATION CHALLENGES AND FUN

Ross felt no place had as much authenticity for *The Hunger Games* as mountainous North Carolina. The drawbacks of the location's authenticity were poor roads, bears appearing at the slightest scent of food, and the weather. Daily rain showers in North Carolina, as well as afternoon and morning shade, limited filming to only four to five hours a day. The film's soundstage was a converted cigarette factory that had an eerie atmosphere, which the cast and crew were glad to leave behind once filming completed.

Heat and humidity intensified the already exhausting action sequences. During one scene, Lawrence had to run along a specific trail through burning and exploding trees. But amidst the confusion, Lawrence frighteningly lost track of which trees would explode. While on a break from filming, Lawrence was shadowboxing with costar Hutcherson. Lawrence accidentally

Lawrence needed archery training to convincingly play Katniss, a skilled hunter.

kicked Hutcherson in the temple, causing a mild concussion and threatening to halt production. Hutcherson was okay, but Lawrence felt so bad she couldn't stop crying.

While the four-month shoot was grueling, nerve-wracking, and almost always hot, Lawrence enjoyed working with Ross, who pushed and challenged her as an actor. She also bonded with the crew and other cast members, having a blast holding sleepovers and playing pranks. Hutcherson, who admits he's a five-year-old at heart, even pranked Lawrence by planting a mangled prop dummy in her bathroom. Both Hutcherson and Hemsworth, who played Gale, became like brothers to Lawrence.

Similar to Katniss, Lawrence was only starting to learn how to play the role of a celebrity. Luckily, with a film still to work on before *The Hunger Games* premiere, she had one last chance to savor a somewhat low profile before facing her image on a giant billboard.

|||||||||||

CAST SUPPORT

Lawrence's work as Katniss Everdeen received high praise from her *Hunger Games* costars. Veteran actor Donald Sutherland, who shared scenes with Lawrence as President Snow, said she is "one of the very best actors working around today."[3] Hutcherson said, "When you are acting with [Lawrence], when you look into her eyes, you see that she is being that character. There is no lying."[4] And Woody Harrelson, who stars as Haymitch, said Lawrence is an actor to watch. "I don't know what will happen for her career, but I can't imagine that it won't go for another 80 years," he said.[5]

Lawrence greets *Hunger Games* fans during a visit to the *Late Show with David Letterman*.

CHAPTER 8

How Far Will She Go?

||||||||||||||||||||||||||||||||||||||||||||||||||

Even with the starring role in a major movie blockbuster like *The Hunger Games*, Lawrence's love for independent films remained. In October 2011, a few months after wrapping *The Hunger Games*, the 21-year-old actress went to Pennsylvania to film the independent movie *The Silver Linings Playbook*. Directed by David O. Russell, the movie stars Bradley Cooper as a former teacher who moves back in with his parents after spending four years in a mental institution. Acting veteran and Oscar winner Robert De Niro stars as Cooper's father. Cooper's character attempts to reconcile with his ex-wife, but becomes smitten with Lawrence's character, Tiffany.

Lawrence wrapped filming on *The Silver Linings Playbook* at the end of 2011. As *The Hunger Games* release drew closer, Lawrence helped share the excitement she experienced the previous year by helping announce the 84th Academy Award nominations on January 24, 2012. Then by February 2012, Lawrence's life had become consumed by all things *Hunger Games*.

HUNGER GAMES HYPE

Like most eagerly anticipated movies, incessant buzz surrounded *The Hunger Games*. Lionsgate utilized social media Web sites such as Twitter, Facebook, and YouTube to reach the series' rapidly growing fan base. The movie's trailer was released on the Internet on November 14, 2011, reaching 8 million views within the first 24 hours of its launch.

During the promotional excitement for the film's March 12, 2012, premiere, insiders were already projecting the film to earn a phenomenal $150 million during its opening weekend. In addition to the eight-city promotional mall tour, Lawrence and her cast mates embarked on a whirlwind press junket that included interviews and public appearances. During one 24-hour period, Lawrence walked down four red carpets in four different gowns.

WEIGHT CRITICISM

Following the release of *The Hunger Games*, some critics created a media storm by making negative comments about Lawrence's weight in the film. Several wrote that it did not reflect her character, Katniss, who comes from a poor district where food is scarce. One critic wrote that the actress had "lingering baby fat,"[1] while another wrote that her "womanly figure makes a bad fit for a dystopian fantasy about a people starved into submission."[2]

But many defended Lawrence, saying the comments about the actress are irresponsible, including body image expert Sarah Maria: "This type of criticism is not just silly, it is damaging."[3] Actor Stanley Tucci, who costars in *The Hunger Games* as Caesar Flickerman, also blasted the comments as "ridiculous." "That's all you can say . . . I think [Lawrence] is great, no matter how big her bones are. And they're not big! She's gorgeous," he said.[4]

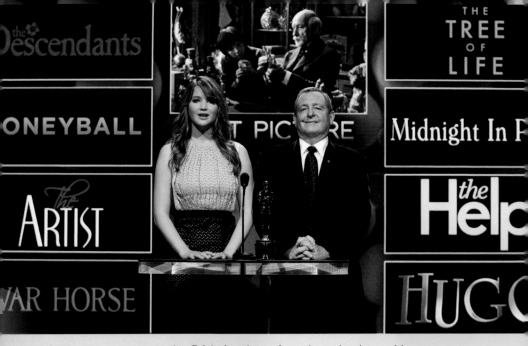

Lawrence announces the 84th Academy Award nominations with Academy president Tom Sherak.

Over the days leading up to *The Hunger Games'* March 23 release, some wondered if Lawrence's self-esteem was starting to show some cracks. During a radio interview on the *Ryan Seacrest Show*, Lawrence said, perhaps jokingly, she was the worst part of *The Hunger Games*. On the *Late Show with David Letterman*, Lawrence made similar comments, saying she didn't like looking at herself onscreen: "I'm a troll. I hate myself. . . . I think the movie is great, but their biggest mistake was me."[5]

Some entertainment writers and bloggers found her attitude refreshing and down-to-earth—she did appear to be joking and laughing during the two interviews. Others, however, were upset that she wasn't more appreciative of her talents. One reporter noted the comments were the opposite of the confident actress who flew to New York to lock down her *Winter's Bone* role and posed for *Esquire* to radically change her image.

Lawrence has admitted in interviews that she has terrible self-esteem. Since her earliest experiences with fame, her discomfort with media attention has been well documented.

STAYING GROUNDED

Fortunately, Lawrence's next film role helped her escape the commotion. Three days after *The Hunger Games* premiere, *Serena* began filming on March 26, 2012, in Prague, Czech Republic. Lawrence signed on for the title role of Serena Pemberton, once again starring opposite *The Silver Linings Playbook* costar Cooper. The foreign setting is a stand-in for Depression-era North Carolina, where the film's drama unfolds. Lawrence plays the wife of Cooper's lumber baron George.

Lawrence has tried to remain grounded by focusing on her career as an actress. This dedication, she has said, follows the example of her parents, who both worked hard on things they were passionate about. Ultimately, Lawrence understands that acting can be an unglamorous job involving insanely long hours and hard work. Lawrence has said she knows becoming successful requires that sort of commitment, and industry insiders have praised her work ethic. *The Hunger Games* director Ross said of Lawrence, "She gets up at 6 a.m., she has a quiet, centered life with a great boyfriend. She's a calm, stable person."[6]

> "Jennifer doesn't have a trace of arrogance. She's not trying to put on airs or be anyone she's not. She's the real deal. She's just this frickin' amazing gal from Kentucky who hit it big."[7]
>
> —*WOODY HARRELSON*

Adding to Lawrence's sense of stability is her intense craving for a normal life, reflecting her normal upbringing. Lawrence cites Foster, her

The Beaver director, as her biggest role model in Hollywood. Lawrence told *The Wall Street Journal*:

> *She's the only person who I've seen who's just so normal. Every time I look at her I say a silent prayer, 'Let me end up that way.' I'm not worried about being nice. I want to be more than nice. I want to be normal.*[8]

DUELING FRANCHISES

Lawrence is committed to future X-Men movies and the Hunger Games sequels. After the success of *The Hunger Games*, Lionsgate immediately started plans for the sequel, *Catching Fire*. Meanwhile, Twentieth Century Fox also planned for its X-Men follow-up. Fox considered a fall of 2012 shoot, and Lionsgate aimed for summer 2012, making schedule conflicts a certainty. But Fox also had an advantage because Lawrence's *X-Men: First Class* contract came before her commitment to the Hunger Games. Disaster was averted, however, when Fox announced on April 5, 2012, it would postpone *X-Men* filming until January 2013. That gave Lionsgate the green light to shoot *Catching Fire*. But the scheduled shooting date left very little time for preproduction work on *Catching Fire*. The rushed production schedule caused Ross to bow out as director. By April 2012, Lionsgate had announced that Francis Lawrence, the director of *Water for Elephants* and *I Am Legend*, had been hired to direct *Catching Fire*.

WAITING FOR WHAT'S NEXT

After *The Hunger Games*, Lawrence has received even more scripts to read. Lawrence has always looked at the script, the character, and the director when considering projects. It doesn't matter to her if they are big features or small independent films. While some actors might take on a role as a challenge, Lawrence has said she selects roles she wants to do and knows she is capable of playing. She has said she feels blessed to have played strong women, rather than the young ingénue parts typically offered to actresses her age.

> "I've never cried over not getting a role. I'm a big believer in what's meant to be will happen. I've watched fate play out so wonderfully without me being in control of it."[9]
>
> —JENNIFER LAWRENCE

Lawrence has shown interest in finding a way to support the causes she feels passionate about. In March 2012, Lawrence appeared in a short film supporting Bellewood Home for Children, which aids abused and neglected youth in her home state of Kentucky. It is an organization that has been very important to Lawrence's family, and her parents have opened up their summer camp to the children at Bellewood. "Bellewood is very close to my heart because it's been in my family for generations," Lawrence said in the film.[10]

And Lawrence also said she wants to find more causes to support, saying, "I've been wanting to get involved with charities working with orphanages in third world countries and other things like that."[11]

But being an actress is just the beginning for Lawrence. Directing is something Lawrence has also expressed an interest in, particularly after receiving "junior" directing lessons from her *Burning Plain* director Guillermo Arriaga during filming. But she's also talked about following in her mother's footsteps, having children and driving a minivan.

Lawrence, who is ever the realist, has said that it is impossible to know what's going to happen next in her career. Ten years ago, she never could have predicted her Academy Award nomination at the age of 20 or landing such a high-profile role as

Lawrence has been reluctant to discuss details whenever interviewers ask about her romantic life. As of June 2012, the media reported that Lawrence was dating her *X-Men: First Class* costar Nicholas Hoult. While Lawrence has joked that they're just basketball buddies, her friend Zoe Kravitz thinks it's a good match. "She's crazy and impulsive, but he keeps her grounded," Kravitz told *Rolling Stone*. "And she keeps him on his toes."[14]

Katniss Everdeen in the Hunger Games franchise. "So in ten years from now, I might be running a rodeo," she told *Flare* magazine.[12]

While anything is possible, Lawrence has remained committed to two franchises—the Hunger Games and X-Men. Outside of the two franchises, many in the industry have predicted that Lawrence will establish a long career. "I think she's peerless in her generation, honest to God," Ross said.[13] That means the girl from Kentucky will be gracing the big screen for a long time to come—much to the delight of her fans.

Lawrence waves to fans at Paris Fashion Week in July 2012.

TIMELINE

1990

Jennifer Shrader Lawrence is born in Louisville, Kentucky, on August 15.

2004

During spring break, a talent scout discovers Jennifer in Union Square, New York City, at age 14.

2004

Jennifer moves to New York over the summer to begin her acting career.

2008

The Burning Plain premieres August 27 at the Venice International Film Festival; Lawrence wins the festival's Marcello Mastroianni Award for best emerging performer.

2009

The Bill Engvall Show is cancelled in September after three seasons on TBS.

2010

Winter's Bone premieres on January 21 at the Sundance Film Festival and wins the festival's Grand Jury Prize.

2006

2007

2008

Jennifer earns her high school diploma at age 16.

Jennifer begins her role as Lauren on the comedy series *The Bill Engvall Show*.

The Poker House premieres June 20 at the Los Angeles Film Festival; Jennifer wins the festival's Outstanding Performance award.

2010

2010

2011

Lawrence films *Like Crazy* in the fall.

X-Men: First Class, Lawrence's first big studio movie, begins filming in England.

Lawrence receives an Academy Award nomination for Best Actress in a Leading Role on January 25.

TIMELINE

2011

Lawrence attends the 83rd Academy Awards on February 27.

2011

Lionsgate announces Lawrence has been cast as Katniss Everdeen in *The Hunger Games* movie in March.

2011

The Hunger Games begins filming in North Carolina.

2012

Lawrence and other *The Hunger Games* cast members participate in an eight-city mall tour.

2012

The Hunger Games movie premieres on March 12 in Los Angeles.

2012

The Hunger Games movie opens in the United States on March 23.

2011

In October, Lawrence shoots *The Silver Linings Playbook* in Pennsylvania.

2011

The Hunger Games trailer is released and gets 8 million views in 24 hours.

2012

Lawrence co-announces the 84th Academy Awards nominations on January 24.

2012

Lawrence begins filming *Serena* in Prague, Czech Republic, at the end of March.

2012

Catching Fire begins filming in August.

2013

The *X-Men: First Class* follow-up begins filming in January.

FULL NAME

Jennifer Shrader Lawrence

DATE OF BIRTH

August 15, 1990

PLACE OF BIRTH

Louisville, Kentucky

SELECTED FILMS AND TELEVISION APPEARANCES

Monk (2006), *Cold Case* (2007), *Medium* (2007, 2008), *The Bill Engvall Show* (2007–2009), *The Poker House* (2008), *The Burning Plain* (2008), *Winter's Bone* (2010), *Like Crazy* (2011), *The Beaver* (2011), *X-Men: First Class* (2011), *The Hunger Games* (2012), *House at the End of the Street* (2012), *The Silver Linings Playbook* (2012)

SELECTED AWARDS AND NOMINATIONS

- Won 2008 Los Angeles Film Festival award for Outstanding Performance for *The Poker House* (2008)
- Won 2008 Venice International Film Festival Marcello Mastroianni Award for best emerging performer for *The Burning Plain* (2008)
- Nominated for 2011 68th Annual Golden Globe Awards for Best Performance by an Actress in a Motion Picture—Drama for *Winter's Bone* (2010)

- Nominated for 2011 17th Annual Screen Actors Guild Awards for Outstanding Performance by a Female Actor in a Leading Role for *Winter's Bone* (2010)
- Nominated for 2011 83rd Academy Awards for Actress in a Leading Role for *Winter's Bone* (2010)

PHILANTHROPY

Lawrence has supported a number of charitable causes, including an appearance in a short film supporting Bellewood Home for Children, which cares for abused, neglected, and homeless children in her native Kentucky. Lawrence also appeared in public service announcements with her *The Hunger Games* cast mates to support the World Food Programme and Feeding America to raise awareness about world hunger.

> "Yeah, I do have big ambitions, but I think we all do. I just want to keep working hard and being happy. . . . There are a lot of things that I know I'm going to learn about myself, because we all do. But yeah, I have big ambitions."
>
> —JENNIFER LAWRENCE

GLOSSARY

audition—To give a trial performance showcasing personal talent as a musician, singer, dancer, or actor.

cold-read—Reading for a part without preparation or rehearsal.

debut—A first appearance.

dystopian—An imagined place with a bleak environment and society.

franchise—A series of films or television shows, including merchandising rights.

genre—A category of art, music, or literature characterized by a particular style, form, or content.

gig—A temporary job.

improvisation—The act of making up an acting scene or comedy skit on the spot, instead of working from a script and rehearsing.

ingénue—An innocent young woman.

paparazzi—Aggressive photojournalists who take pictures of celebrities and sell them to media outlets.

premiere—The first public showing.

preproduction—The work done before a movie is filmed.

prequel—A story or movie with events that come before a previously made story or movie.

self-deprecating—Being critical of oneself.

sequel—A story or movie with events that come after a previously made story or movie.

sitcom—A television comedy series, shortened from "situation comedy."

stage parent—A mother or father who is overly involved in their child's performing career.

starstruck—Being in awe of famous people.

typecast—Being associated with a single kind of acting role.

wrap—When movie filming finishes.

ADDITIONAL RESOURCES

SELECTED BIBLIOGRAPHY

Balfour, Brad. "Best Actress Nominee Jennifer Lawrence Heat Up 'Winter's Bone.'" *Huffington Post*. Huffington Post. 25 Feb. 2011. Web. 26 Mar. 2012.

Eells, Josh. "America's Kick-Ass Sweetheart. (Cover Story)." *Rolling Stone* 1154 (2012): 38. *MasterFILE Premier*. Web. 16 Aug. 2012.

Moss, Josh. "Too Young For Methods." *Louisville Magazine* 61.12 (2010): 37–40. *MasterFILE Premier*. Web. 30 July 2012.

FURTHER READINGS

Gresh, Lois H. *The Hunger Games Companion: The Unauthorized Guide to the Series*. New York: St. Martin's, 2011. Print.

Seife, Emily. *The Hunger Games Tribute Guide*. New York: Scholastic, 2012. Print.

WEB SITES

To learn more about Jennifer Lawrence, visit ABDO
Publishing Company online at **www.abdopublishing.com**.
Web sites about Jennifer Lawrence are featured on our
Book Links page. These links are routinely monitored and
updated to provide the most current information available.

PLACES TO VISIT

Asheville Visitor Center
36 Montford Avenue, Asheville, NC 28801
828-258-6129
www.exploreasheville.com/
Hike and explore *The Hunger Games* filming locations in the
Blue Ridge Mountains.

Louisville Visitors Center
301 South Fourth Street, Louisville, KY 40202
Toll-free call center: 1-888-568-4784
www.gotolouisville.com/index.aspx
Check out where Jennifer Lawrence grew up by visiting
her hometown.

Shiloh Museum of Ozark History
118 W. Johnson Avenue, Springdale, AR 72764
479-750-8165
www.shilohmuseum.org/
Get a taste of Ozark life as experienced by the characters in
Winter's Bone.

SOURCE NOTES

CHAPTER 1. READY FOR FAME?

1. Bryan Alexander. "Lawrence Isn't Swayed by Fame Game." *USA Today.* 23 Mar. 2012. *MasterFILE Premier.* 26 Mar. 2012.

2. John Green. "Scary New World." *New York Times.* New York Times, 9 Nov. 2008. Web. 26 July 2012.

3. "Jennifer Lawrence on Josh Hutcherson's Rating of Her Kissing Skills and Hunger Games 'Pressure.'" *YouTube.* YouTube, 12 Mar. 2012. Web. 2 Apr. 2012.

4. Karen Valby. "The Chosen One." *Entertainment Weekly.* Entertainment Weekly, 20 May 2011. Web. 26 Mar. 2012.

5. Ibid.

6. "First Look at Jennifer Lawrence as Katniss in 'The Hunger Games.'" *Entertainment Weekly.* Entertainment Weekly, 18 May 2011. Web. 26 Mar. 2012.

7. Dana Stevens. "The Hunger Games: Just Go See It." *Slate.* Slate, 22 Mar. 2012. Web. 9 Apr. 2012.

8. Peter Travers. "The Hunger Games." *Rolling Stone.* Rolling Stone, 21 Mar. 2012. Web. 26 Mar. 2012.

9. Michael Phillips. "'The Hunger Games' Adaptation Hits the Target." *Chicago Tribune.* Chicago Tribune, 20 Mar. 2012. Web. 9 Apr. 2012.

10. David Edelstein. "Movie Review: The Slick Hunger Games Purges All the Horror." *New York Magazine.* New York Media, 22 Mar. 2012. Web. 9 Apr. 2012.

CHAPTER 2. DISCOVERED IN THE BIG APPLE

1. Iona Kirby and Hugo Daniel. "Fresh-Faced Hunger Games Star Jennifer Lawrence Pictured before She Was Famous." *Mail Online.* Daily Mail, 29 Mar. 2012. Web. 26 July 2012.

2. Josh Eells. "America's Kick-Ass Sweetheart. (Cover Story)." *Rolling Stone* 1154 (2012): 38. *MasterFILE Premier.* Web. 16 Aug. 2012.

3. Josh Moss. "Too Young For Methods." *Louisville Magazine* 61.12 (2010): 37. *MasterFILE Premier.* Web. 30 July 2012.

4. "Jennifer Lawrence 2011 Oscar Luncheon Interview by Access Hollywood." *YouTube.* YouTube, 9 Oct. 2011. Web. 5 Apr. 2012.

CHAPTER 3. SMALL AND BIG SCREEN ROLES

1. Alan Baltes. "Jennifer Lawrence Discusses Her Dramatic Work as an Actress, How She Chooses Her Roles, and How She Foresees Her Career Progressing." *Examiner.* Clarity Digital Group, 13 Mar. 2012. Web. 30 July 2012.

2. Joseph Lord. "Jennifer Lawrence: Bigger Things." *Metromix Louisville*. Metromix, 14 Oct. 2009. Web. 30 July 2012.

3. Jason Guerrasio. "Jennifer Lawrence Q&A." *FilmMaker Magazine*. FilmMaker Magazine, 26 Feb. 2011. Web. 30 July 2012.

4. Amanda Luttrell Garrigus. "Girl on Fire." *Flare*. Vol. 33 Issue 6. Jun 2011. *MasterFILE Premier*. 26 Mar. 2012.

CHAPTER 4. A BREAKOUT PERFORMANCE

1. Jason Guerrasio. "Jennifer Lawrence Q&A." *FilmMaker Magazine*. FilmMaker Magazine, 26 Feb. 2011. Web. 30 July 2012.

2. Alan Baltes. "Jennifer Lawrence Discusses Her Dramatic Work as an Actress, How She Chooses Her Roles, and How She Foresees Her Career Progressing." *Examiner*. Clarity Digital Group, 13 Mar. 2012. Web. 30 July 2012.

3. Josh Moss. "Too Young For Methods." *Louisville Magazine* 61.12 (2010): 37–40. *MasterFILE Premier*. Web. 30 July 2012.

4. Reed Johnson. "Jennifer Lawrence, Playing to Strength." *Los Angeles Times*. Los Angeles Times, 11 Nov. 2010. Web. 30 July 2012.

5. Josh Moss. "Too Young For Methods." *Louisville Magazine* 61.12 (2010): 37–40. *MasterFILE Premier*. Web. 30 July 2012.

6. "Winter's Bone (4 of 5)." *YouTube*. YouTube, 03 June 2010. Web. 30 July 2012.

CHAPTER 5. FROM GRITTY TO GLAM

1. A.O. Scott. "Where Life Is Cold, and Kin Are Cruel." *New York Times*. New York Times, 10 June 2010. Web. 25 Apr. 2012.

2. Peter Travers. "Winter's Bone–Movie Reviews." *Rolling Stone*. Rolling Stone, 3 June 2010. Web. 30 July 2012.

3. "Jennifer Lawrence 2." *YouTube*. YouTube, 27 Oct. 2010. Web. 30 July 2012.

4. "Enjoying the Hunger Games Ride." *Sydney Morning Herald*. Fairfax Media, 13 May 2012. Web. 16 Aug. 2012.

5. Josh Moss. "Too Young For Methods." *Louisville Magazine* 61.12 (2010): 37–40. *MasterFILE Premier*. Web. 30 July 2012.

6. Jeremy Medina. "Jennifer Lawrence Dishes on 'Winter's Bone' and Stripping for 'Esquire.'" *BlackBook*. BlackBook, 28 June 2010. Web. 30 July 2012.

7. Nicole Sperling. "Jennifer Lawrence: In 'Hunger Games,' a Heroine for Our Times." *Los Angeles Times*. Latimes.com. 16 Mar. 2012. Web. 26 Mar. 2012.

8. Jeremy Medina. "Jennifer Lawrence Dishes on 'Winter's Bone' and Stripping for 'Esquire.'" *BlackBook*. BlackBook, 28 June 2010. Web. 30 July 2012.

9. "Jennifer Lawrence 2." *YouTube*. YouTube, 27 Oct. 2010. Web. 30 July 2012.

10. Karen Valby. "The Chosen One." *Entertainment Weekly*. Entertainment Weekly, 20 May 2011. Web. 26 Mar. 2012.

CHAPTER 6. A TRIP TO THE OSCARS

1. Melena Ryzik. "The Education of a Newbie." *New York Times*. New York Times, 16 Jan. 2011. Web. 30 July 2012.

2. Joseph Lord. "Louisville's Jennifer Lawrence Waits for Magical Oscar Nomination." *Louisville Courier-Journal*. Louisville Courier-Journal, 23 Jan. 2011. Web. 27 Mar. 2012.

3. "Celebrity Jennifer Lawrence on Access Hollywood." *YouTube*. YouTube, 29 Jan. 2011. Web. 30 July 2012.

4. Ibid.

5. Joseph Lord. "Louisville's Jennifer Lawrence Waits for Magical Oscar Nomination." *Louisville Courier-Journal*. Louisville Courier-Journal, 23 Jan. 2011. Web. 27 Mar. 2012.

6. "Celebrity Jennifer Lawrence on Access Hollywood." *YouTube*. YouTube, 29 Jan. 2011. Web. 30 July 2012.

7. Melissa Magsaysay. "Oscars: Calvin Klein's Red Carpet Reign Continues." *Los Angeles Times*. Los Angeles Times, 27 Feb. 2011. Web. 5 Apr. 2012.

8. Josh Moss. "Too Young For Methods." *Louisville Magazine* 61.12 (2010): 37–40. *MasterFILE Premier*. Web. 30 July 2012.

CHAPTER 7. TAKING ON *THE HUNGER GAMES*

1. Stephen Galloway. "The High Stakes Behind 'Hunger Games.'" *Hollywood Reporter*. Hollywood Reporter, 1 Feb. 2012. Web. 27 Mar. 2012.

2. "First Look at Jennifer Lawrence as Katniss in 'The Hunger Games.'" *Entertainment Weekly*. Entertainment Weekly, 18 May 2011. Web. 26 Mar. 2012.

3. Silas Lesnick. "Donald Sutherland on the Sociopolitical Importance of The Hunger Games." *ComingSoon.net*. CraveOnline Media, 14 Mar. 2012. Web. 30 July 2012.

4. Nicole Sperling. "Jennifer Lawrence: In 'Hunger Games,' a Heroine for Our Times." *Los Angeles Times*. Los Angeles Times, 16 Mar. 2012. Web. 26 Mar. 2012.

5. Alicia Rancilio. "'Hunger Games' Support Cast Wowed by Story, Star." *Yahoo! News*. Yahoo, 22 Mar. 2012. Web. 30 July 2012.

CHAPTER 8. HOW FAR WILL SHE GO?

1. Alex Rees. "Some Movie Critics Were Unhappy With Jennifer Lawrence's 'Baby Fat' in The Hunger Games." *New York Magazine*. New York Media, 27 Mar. 2012. Web. 30 July 2012.

2. Ibid.

3. Ibid.

4. Ibid.

5. "Video: Jennifer Lawrence on 'David Letterman.'" *The Hob*. Thehob.org, 21 Mar. 2012. Web. 30 July 2012.

6. Bryan Alexander. "Lawrence Isn't Swayed by Fame Game." *USA Today*, 23 Mar. 2012. *MasterFILE Premier*. Web. 26 Mar. 2012.

7. Josh Eells. "America's Kick-Ass Sweetheart. (Cover Story)." *Rolling Stone* 1154 (2012): 38. *MasterFILE Premier*. Web. 16 Aug. 2012.

8. John Jurgensen. "Unnerved by a Taste of Fame." *Wall Street Journal*. Wall Street Journal, 27 May 2011. Web. 11 Apr. 2012.

9. Jay A. Fernandez. "Jennifer Lawrence: The Making of an 'It' Actress." *Hollywood Reporter*. Hollywood Reporter, 19 Jan. 2011. Web. 12 Apr. 2012.

10. "Jennifer Lawrence Promotes Bellewood in Short Film." *Bellewood*. Bellewood Home for Children, 7 Mar. 2012. Web. 30 July 2012.

11. Izumi Hasegawa. "Film Interview: Jennifer Lawrence." *Buzzine*. Buzzine, 20 Mar. 2012. Web. 30 July 2012.

12. Amanda Luttrell Garrigus. "Girl On Fire." *Flare* 33.6 (2011): 126. *MasterFILE Premier*. Web. 30 July 2012.

13. Jim Slotek. "Lawrence in Awe of 'Hunger' Fans." *Toronto Sun*. Canoe Sun Media, 18 Mar. 2012. Web. 30 July 2012.

14. Josh Eells. "America's Kick-Ass Sweetheart. (Cover Story)." *Rolling Stone* 1154 (2012): 38. *MasterFILE Premier*. Web. 16 Aug. 2012.

INDEX

110

ABOUT THE AUTHOR

Melissa Higgins is the author of many nonfiction books for children and young adults, writing on topics ranging from appreciating diversity to biographies of people in the news. She also writes short stories and novels. Before pursuing a writing career, Ms. Higgins worked as a mental-health counselor in schools and private practice.

PHOTO CREDITS